SUPERVILLAINS WITH BADGES

WE'RE ON A HITLIST

TRAITORS, POSERS, SELLOUTS, MURDERERS

Theresa & Tess Nichols

Supervillains with Badges – We're on a Hitlist: Traitors, Posers, Sellouts, Murderers

Copyright © 2024 by Theresa and Tess Nichols

No portion of this book may be reproduced in any form without written permission from the publisher or author, except as permitted by U.S. copyright law. This publication is designed to provide accurate and authoritative information in regard to the subject matter covered. Readers acknowledge that this work is sold with the understanding that neither the author nor the publisher is engaging in the rendering of legal, financial, medical, political, or professional advice. The content has been derived from various sources; consult with a professional when appropriate. Every attempt has been made to provide accurate, up to date and reliable complete information. While the publisher and author have used their best efforts in preparing this book, they make no representations or warranties with respect to the accuracy or completeness of the contents of this book and specifically disclaim any implied warranties of merchantability or fitness for a particular purpose. The advice and strategies contained herein may not be suitable for your situation. Neither the publisher nor the author shall be liable for any loss of profit or any other commercial damages, including but not limited to special, incidental, consequential, personal, or other damages.

Scriptures are taken from the Geneva Bible 1560, public domain.

Library of Congress Control Number: 2024923831

ISBNs
978-1-958978-27-6 IngramSpark Paperback
978-1-958978-28-3 KDP Paperback
978-1-985978-30-6 KDP eBook

1st edition 2024

All Rights Reserved

Contents

Prologue . . . V

Dedication . . . VII

1. How It All Began . . . 1

2. The Trigger . . . 7

3. Tag! You're It! . . . 15

4. Airtags Found . . . 19

5. We're Not Spooked . . . 23

6. Tailed, Surveilled and Threatened . . . 27

7. It's Unlawful! . . . 31

8. Feds in the Sky . . . 37
(The Little Cessna That Couldn't)

9. A Busy 3 Weeks . . . 43

10. The Red Bat Phone . . . 47

11. Rope . . . 51

12. Feds at Our Door	55
13. Attempted Kidnapping	61
14. Feds Online	71
15. Open Investigation	75
16. Why the Tyrants Rage	77
Epilogue	81
Acknowledgements	87
About the Authors	89

Prologue

Enduring flyovers, airtags, dirt boxes, stingrays, trespassing, attempted kidnapping, surveillance, misdirecting and device manipulation, unresponsive and blocked 911 calls, wiretapping, false accusations, mail theft, extortion, fraud, impersonations, and stalking, yet we are unmoved.

This is our truthful account, our witness, our sworn testimony of what the federal government does to anyone they hate because they oppose their narrative and have intel on their criminality. Our Barry addressed a card to me as the mother of his very heart. He apologized that my being there for him has made me a target for these evil fed bastards! Like Barry, I made a choice and counted the cost back in 2020. Just being there for Barry has cost me the peace and sanctity of my daily life. It has brought this evil federal government, who call themselves the good guys, into my life, and the life of my daughter. I will not stand for their targeting of my precious and virtuous daughter. They have crossed the line if they come nigh unto her.

But let us tell you of our gains for having answered Father's call. We have gained the protection of God's angels and eternal rewards to cast at our Alpha Jesus' feet. We have gained Truth, Light and Understanding. We have gained courage and determination. We have gained discernment and can spot a fed and their paid contractors from miles away. Best of all, my daughter gained a husband, and I gained a son. Together, we will serve the Living God in our mortal clay for the rest of our natural lives. We three are eternal spirits bound together for Father's purposes through His Son Jesus Christ for all eternity and all dimensions.

Thank you, Barry, for your expression of sorrow for me. No apologies necessary, It is an honor to serve you, my daughter, and Father. The three of us were chosen to be in this fight for Father's glory. Sir, it has been an honor serving with you. Standard operating procedure change: Secure and hold perimeter. Roger that.

Dedication

And they overcame him because of the blood of the Lamb and because of the word of their testimony, and they did not love their life even when faced with death.

And he showed me a pure river of water of life, clear as crystal, proceeding out of the throne of God, and of the Lamb.

Revelation 12:11; 22: 1

How It All Began

My journey with Barry Gordon Croft, Jr. began with a desperate plea to Father. (That's how I address God.) "Father! How could a free Republic be forced to follow mandates? How could this be happening? What about our Constitution?" I begged Father to reveal to me what was really happening in America. I knew it was a demonic tsunami. I had been warned of that in my spirit in late 2019, but I needed it explained to me. I knew it would mean finding the River of God, but even that was unclear to my awakening mind.

I was scrolling through my Facebook live feed when my eye was caught by a man in a tricorn hat speaking of the Constitution and the rights of all men before God. Instantly, I knew that this man had the answers I sought.

I learned that the Constitution is defunct and a new de facto document had taken its place, the United States Code (USC), and it contained many thousands of pages. It was ever in flux, as agencies add to it and change it on the daily. This de facto document, although illegitimate, is in effect. In it, I found that Presidential powers have been delegated to agencies at will, and that is why the CDC could mandate our lives. In fact, any agency can mandate our lives! Faceless, unaccountable, unelected bureaucrats had taken the place of "We the People," and are now in charge. Not you, not your vote, not Congress. No. The agencies run this country and they can do whatever the heck they want. America is a bureaucracy. Three branches have been merged into one dictatorship. The truth had burst through my mind and it all made sense. Truth has a way of doing that.

Barry and I became friends. I would speak to him often on the phone and by text. We talked tirelessly about faith and freedom. After our talks, I'd go straight to researching everything we discussed. I grew in my understanding and truth began to flood my mind. I grew in understanding, discernment, wisdom, and faith. I became physically stronger and my mind gained a steel that I could not explain, except that truth can literally transform the mind, soul, body, and spirit. I had finally come to know what was happening in this country, and Father called me up to serve Him.

My service to Father would be to stand by Barry and not leave him. I could sense a persecution was coming for him and Father wanted me to help him through it. I said, "Yes" to Father. I would help Barry and not leave him. In fact, I'm still doing just that at the writing of this book. The demonic tsunami had made contact with American shores and the plans of psychopathic elites became public in March 2020, when mask mandates and social distancing were put in effect because of a virus. Lockdowns destroyed businesses and homes. The long term effects would destroy the supply chain and workforce. Then a poisonous depopulation "vaccine" created by the Department of Defense would be mandated into the veins of a naive and distorted public. This would be the backdrop of a staged act of terrorism and lying plot perpetrated on Barry.

Barry Croft Jr. is a Christian Constitutionalist. So am I. So is my daughter. He was being pursued by the federal government because of his KNOWLEDGE. He knew, firsthand, that they had killed his friend and fellow Christian Constitutionalist, KC M. Barry knows of the murders that federal agents commit and how they hire evil men to make their hits. The feds killed KC because he exposed their crimes at our country's southern border. He recorded the feds coming over the border with illegals and drugs. KC captured the crime on his night vision goggles and posted it on Facebook. A hit was sent out to get him. A wicked, fed-filled motorcycle gang captured, tortured and killed KC in seclusion in Texas. His body was thrown on the side of the road and a Confidential Human Source (CHS) hired by the feds, sent photos of KC's dead body to Barry. They also sent recordings of KC screaming as they tortured him. Barry still has nightmares. Now the feds wanted to kill Barry. They did not succeed, but they did succeed in putting him in a concrete box in the USP Florence ADMAX. He's innocent. When that comes out, and it will, because truth cannot be silenced forever, you will have a choice to make, America. Keep your head buried up your rear or grow a pair and decide never to comply with governmental tyranny again. This will not just go away. The New World Order has been the plan for centuries and the evil elitists in charge of global control are at work right now. My daughter and I have found that this global tyranny is hard at work right in the community where we live. Agencies and law enforcement combined with weaponized medicine and health facilities have all teamed up to create lying plots to capture and murder any dissenting voice.

For the record, we will not comply with governmental tyranny. We can coexist with these monsters, but if they crossover into our God-given jurisdiction to Life, Liberty and the Pursuit of Happiness, we will resist with our lives. We will speak truth. This is the only way the demonic tsunami can be stopped. Truth combined with actions that say, "I will not comply with wicked mandates that contradict my basic freedoms given to me by God."

The true story of our lives and what has happened to us start here. We have followed Barry through it all. You can read about our journey with Barry through his arrest and trials in our first book, "Whitmer Kidnapping Hoax: A Plot to Kidnap Barry Croft Jr. Nameless Casualties, Secret Wars." Loving, admiring, supporting, and helping Barry has put us on a hitlist. Don't worry. You are on one too. The feds want to exterminate you as well and, make no mistake, you are scheduled for demolition. It's just when and how. You can line up for your own extermination. Many have already done this. Fear is unamerican and fear has made many line up and do what the government has told them to do. Not us. The hitlist we're on is because we insist on our God given freedom and we will not back down on our love and support of Barry. He did the right thing. He counted the cost and made a full sacrifice of his freedom to expose the criminality of the federal government. All our heroes went to prison. Truth is a hot branding iron. It torments evil. Count the cost. Pay the price. It's only your soul at stake.

The Trigger

The Bureau of Prisons informed us through the Special Investigative Services Technician within the Florence ADMAX that they are opening a full investigation on us because we continue to place money on Barry's commissary account for essentials and food. It seems that our $100 a month is suspect and must be "from nefarious and ill-gotten gains." This kind of criminal abuse placed upon the loved ones of inmates in this insane gulag of solitary confinement must be exposed and prosecuted to the full extent of the law. Just as the psychopaths are in charge of the psych wards, the criminals are in charge of prisons. Our hatred for one another is mutual.

This is our story of the lengths the federal government, law enforcement, and third party contractors are willing to go to terrorize and commit crimes, with murderous intent, against us. Our insane hatred for the Bureau of Prisons (BOP) is warranted and just. It was triggered on September 21, 2023. Our Barry was supposed to call us on the 19th of September but no call came from USP Terre Haute in Indiana. He had worked hard to get our phone numbers on his approved call list. The BOP resisted and would not give the necessary paperwork to make that change. Barry is resourceful and tenacious and took matters into his own righteous hands. He had fellow inmates "fish" the necessary paperwork down the range in exchange for food. He also protected the men's possessions from the junkies on the range by safekeeping everything from those who would steal it. He was paid with stamps so he could write to us, as well as the paperwork for the approved call list. The men used to say, "Croft, don't you want food instead of stamps? Aren't ya hungry? "Nay." he replied. "I've got a beautiful lady and she likes receiving my letters." With the paperwork filed, we were on his approved call list.

Along with the documentation was an Intent to Marry form. We had worked very hard to get all the documents that the Bureau of Prisons requires to make that happen. He talked to the prison chaplain, the counselor, and unit team manager and wanted to set a date for his marriage to my daughter, Tessie Liz. Everything was in order, just as policy dictates, with all expenses paid.

The chaplain officiates all marriages, twice a year, July and December. Barry was set for December. He asked the counselor in charge to set a date. Barry had enough time to marry his beloved before he was scheduled to be sent to the USP Florence ADMAX in Colorado. He was in the process of appealing placement in the ADMAX because only psychotic serial killers that kill guards and inmates go there. That Administrative Remedy would be in process throughout December. Barry says, "Can we set a date to be married?" The counselor replied, "No." Barry said, "Why? I'm going to be here until December. We have time." The counselor abruptly responds, "No. You won't be here in December." He walked away from our Barry. We would learn what that would mean later. Remember, prison's hire psychopathic serial killers paid with taxpayer money.

At least the approved call list included our names now and all that remained for Barry was to count down the hours until September 19th. He longed to tell my daughter that he loves her for the first time on the phone in plain English. The day came and went. No call. This is a particularly brutal prison. Barry is an innocent man on death row. Every form of debauchery exists there. Torture and cage matches with the sound of murder filling the air, coming closer and closer every night. In just a short 6 months in that vile prison, 8 murders happened with guards not only present, but supplying the jagged pieces of metal and rusty lawnmower blades. Hearing the repeated stabbing, 30 thrusts into the body of an inmate, leaves an impression.

   We would wait all day and all night with no call. It was on September 21st that the phone finally rang. We were busy with activities for Barry. It was the dinner hour, 5:41 P.M., when the call came. Tessie's phone rang. We were on the couch. We jumped up and sought a private, quiet part of the house to speak to him. My daughter could hardly wait for the loving exchange they both had planned. She immediately addressed him in her love language, "Gunboat?" She expected to hear the names he had made for her, which are many, and are filled with extreme love and adoration. Instead, there was a long pause of silence as though his brain had short circuited. This 15 minute call was with her fiance, who could not remember her name. This man with an eidetic memory, could not remember her name. He couldn't remember his case. He couldn't remember his evening meal. He could only remember one thing, "I love you."

   As her mother, my brain went into overdrive. What was wrong with Barry? Was this some sort of BOP joke? Was it AI? Or was our Barry poisoned? Did they drug him for our call to hurt him and us, because they didn't want him to have the calls with us in the first place? After the call ended, the trauma began. I had to figure out what had happened to him.

He was in mortal danger and my mother's heart and spirit knew it. Within a half hour, I knew what I had to do. I had to report it. I dialed 911.

"This is 911." I said, "I want to report a possible poisoning in the Bureau of Prisons, USP Terre Haute." I told them Barry Croft Jr. (Identification Number) has been poisoned and I fear for his life. I told them he is to be my son in law and he is incoherent and I suspect he's been poisoned by the prison. It was then I was transferred to a completely different agent. I reexplained the situation and asked for an officer to come to my home for a full report. They promised to come right away. No one came.

I waited with the front porch light on. For almost an hour, I waited, and waited. My Momma spirit knew they were not coming. I called 911 again. I got a different dispatcher. A woman's voice this time. I explained why I called the first time. I told her no officer came to my home as promised. She asked if my address was taken. I said that I didn't remember giving it to the agent the first time. She was very accommodating and very troubled as to why no officer came to receive my report. She had me on hold and when she returned, she had a different tone. Abruptly she transferred me to another agent.

The agent was a terrible man with a mission that was meant to scare and derail me. It did neither. He addressed me as

"Cathy," and informed me that he couldn't come out and I would have to wait. He said, "I can't come to your house today." I told him I wanted to make a report and he wanted me to talk to him on the phone. I told him that I didn't trust him and that I wanted him to come to my home where I would make an in-person report. He laughed at me and said, "You don't trust me?" I said, "No. I don't. Come to my door and I will give my statement." I hung up and waited all night. No calls. No visits. Nothing. I made my third 911 call and it was blocked! As I dialed it, the emergency number was unavailable and blocked from my using it. We have not been able to use that emergency number since then. I knew no one would be coming…ever.

A few days later, I found a voicemail planted in my cell phone. A call from our local police department with a non local police department number. This sinister, diabolical, criminal joint activity of local law enforcement and the Federal Bureau of Investigation planted a bogus voicemail that never happened! They can delete, add, alter and change technology at will!

Thanks to the cops and agents, they have convinced us of their unlawful involvement to cover up an attempted murder in the Bureau of Prisons. We have lived an outstanding life of faith and peace with our fellow man for our entire lives. We are grateful to God for showing us, firsthand, the corruption running this demonic empire called America. Our conclusion of this event is simple. The Feds want Croft dead.

The Lord rebuke all of you involved in pursuing our innocent Barry. Your names are on God's hitlist. Sooner or later, He's gonna cut you down.

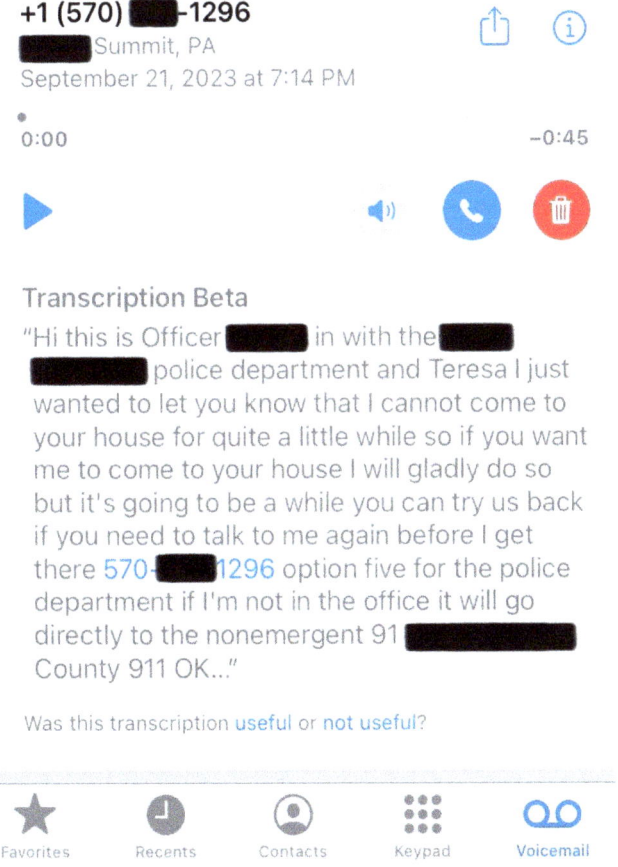

Voicemail placed into device for 911 calls about poisoning in the Bureau of Prisons. The officer never came.

Tag! You're It!

It's been confirmed. We're tagged. Criminal, warrantless, and covertly tagged by "law" enforcement. Supervillains with badges. Cops and agents are working together, seamlessly, in the most criminal syndicate on the planet, America. The American government is at war with her own people.

After a trespasser was located in the shrubs on our property, we undertook researching why. Upon first discovering this paid contractor for the federal government on our property, a sinister cackling could be heard. The visible paid fed was riding a small red farmall type tractor, and his unskilled senses dictated to silence the engine and hide behind our willow tree. As this was happening a tractor trailer air horn was alerting the fellow fed that the homeowners were approaching his location. My beloved daughter had come upon them and they were caught in the act of criminal trespassing. My daughter immediately notified me, and I came storming out the kitchen door. After warning them that they had taken their lives into their own stupid hands for federal debt notes, I returned to the kitchen to get my glock. I screamed, "Get off! Get off!" as loud as my lungs and voice box could achieve. The warning echoed throughout the country valley in which I have peacefully and privately lived for over 35 years. I then unloaded my glock into the woods where the sound of panicked footsteps could be heard.

We weren't done. We got into our car and went in search of the criminal in our yard. We went up the dirt road. It was from there that the sound of the tractor trailer air horn originated. When we arrived to inspect the dirt road, we found a full house of weird people. Two adult women stood there beside a pickup truck in which a man was hiding with his rear end towards us, and a child in the back looking out the truck window. Add to this unlikely and insane scenario, four to five men were standing in the entrance of a large garage. We announced to the out of place women that we were looking for a trespasser that had just been caught on our property. Inappropriate laughter burst forth from the two brain dead women. The man in the truck, like an ostrich, kept his head buried in the cab but forgot about his rear end sticking right out at us. He was hiding again but could be seen. We K-turned our car in front of the women. As we started moving away from them, the trespasser thought he was safe to come out to see us. My daughter has eyes like an eagle and saw him with her 20/20 vision. It was the trespasser!

Airtags Found

We reported the criminal trespassing, but the police did not come, nor did they do the necessary followup required to make an official incident report. After a month of visits to the police station, phone calls, and emails, the officer who was responding to our constant request for a face to face incident report, finally sent us an incomplete form via email. It was peppered with spelling mistakes, grammar errors, missing signatures, and identifying licenses or social security numbers. In fact, the first incident report contained a conclusion that the officer made and not us. He concluded that the reason the trespasser may have been in the center of our property was because the stalker was unsure of the property lines. He had disregarded the fact that the trespasser was hiding behind our willow tree, in the CENTER of our property, having abruptly turned off his tractor's engine. He was hiding.

We now knew that the police and paid federal contractors up on the dirt road were working together to do something criminal. Perhaps several homes had banded together to spy and get paid for it. It's happened before, you know. Neighbors spying on and selling out neighbors. We seem to recall Nazi Germany had this crap going on. What had happened to our neighbors that would induce them to spy on their peaceful neighbors? How could people turn on their blood relatives and long standing neighbors? Why would federal reserve debt notes appeal more to them than truth and clean, honest living? WHY? Like we said, our family has been on this property for 35 years. We own it and raised two children here that have grown to adulthood and are hard working, responsible citizens. We had to find out the answer ourselves. What the heck were these Contractors, also known as Confidential Human Sources (CHS), doing on our property? We went to work. You know what we found? Almost two dozen WiFi networks on our property just beyond our creek, right where that stalker was hiding. Not only were there human tracks in the weeds and bushes, there were WiFi signals and some were cameras and air tags designated for our vehicles. It made complete sense now why the police would not respond to our calls and visits. We knew this already but we enjoy making paper trails of their criminality and calling them out on it. Broadcasting what they do before they do it deters them. The criminals are policing themselves. Justice will not happen here. No. Instead, we give them opportunities to heap judgment on themselves. We give them enough rope to hang themselves before God. We give them the opportunity to stoke their own fires in the bowels of Hell. That's why we stand firm and hold our ground. It's our ground. God gave us jurisdiction over this little two plus acre property and we mean to keep it safe and secure from all invaders, foreign and domestic.

We knew we were being followed for a long time and now we have the proof. These stupid moronic criminals "keep getting dumber and dumber every day" as one of the big fat federal pigs said to my daughter the day he pinned her against the brick post office building. With his big, ugly unmarked federal vehicle, stuffed with his demonic high tech tracking, Momma confronted him and told him to mind his own f-ing business and he got the only hand gesture suitable for such hellbound men. His profession has taught him to return the gesture. It was a good day. We understand each other.

> 3:31 ... LTE
>
> ‹ Settings   Wi-Fi
>
> Wi-Fi   ⬤
>
> MY NETWORKS
>
> TP-Link_DC7█   🔒 📶 ⓘ
>
> OTHER NETWORKS
>
> [range]_E30AJT7113278█ 🔒 📶 ⓘ
>
> ARLO_VMB_532234896█   🔒 📶 ⓘ
>
> ESP_8CA97█   📶 ⓘ
>
> NETGEAR0█   🔒 📶 ⓘ
>
> NETGEAR3█   🔒 📶 ⓘ
>
> NETGEAR4█   🔒 📶 ⓘ
>
> Verizon_4NB9F█   🔒 📶 ⓘ
>
> Verizon_63XDQ█   🔒 📶 ⓘ
>
> Verizon_63XDQ█-Guest   🔒 📶 ⓘ
>
> Other...
>
> Ask to Join Networks   Notify ›

Networks which are airtags, stingrays, dirtboxes, and surveillance cameras in our wooded acre. The ESP was activated by "ethical hacker" and sexual deviant "M." See Chapter 12, "Feds at Our Door."

We're Not Spooked

The couple dozen WiFi networks in our backyard turned out to be a Dirt Box (DRT Box or Digital Receiver Technology.) These are used by law enforcement and federal agents to surveil, track, wiretap and jam phones. That's exactly what happened to us on October 4, 2024 as we were waiting for our beloved Barry to call us from the USP Florence ADMAX. At the time we expected him to call, our phones went dead. They locked up and would not text, call, or receive a call. The keypad to dial locked up and squealed when we attempted to dial a number. A jamming device had been activated.

We are not going to take any of this federal criminality lying down. No. We are not the kind of women that take abuse from anyone, especially not our government! We would not collapse in a heap and sob the victim. We undertook our own investigation.

We left the house immediately and traveled to see the reach of this criminal Dirt Box. As we traveled down our road, it traveled with us. THEN, as we reached the end of the rural route, the phones unlocked. We were outside the range of their surveillance technology.

We decided to spend the day at the park. It was the perfect place to wait for our Barry's call. It was a rare day in Pennsylvania. Clear blue skies and cool air that was warmed by the sun. It was uncommonly hot. It was an unseasonably hot October day, but no one seemed to mind. Everyone was playing, running, biking and conversing. Yes, conversing, but mostly on phones! That is exactly what we needed.

We spent many hours in the park waiting and learning what we were actually up against with governmental corruption and criminality. We found out that we had someone waiting for us in the park.

A man imposed himself in our conversation with the order taker at the park's snack shack. We were talking about coffee when this man interjected into our interaction with the server. We noticed him as soon as we approached the snack shack. He had eyes on us like he was waiting and watching for us to arrive and approach to order.

We knew immediately he was a government agent; a stupid, moronic piece of crap that cared more about federal reserve debt notes and his pride than about the country he bragged to have served his whole life. He let us know the decades he served in the Army and Defense Logistics Agency. We immediately said, "We're sorry to hear that." We wanted to communicate that he had wasted his life doing evil against a free Republic. He then told us, "I'm a patriot," to which we responded, "We're Christian Constitutionalists." He bragged of his pension and life experiences and told us that we would not have the same opportunities because of the economic crisis about to come on younger Americans. We urged him to spend his federal reserve debt notes fast because digital currency is coming and his debt notes will be worthless.

He got bored with us and found out that we didn't believe in his politics and didn't think the vote counted. We gave him no emotion to feed on, just facts. He didn't think the Democratic selected candidate was up to the challenge but he hates the returning Republican selected candidate. We didn't care. Both political parasites. Both will lead us to the precipice of tyranny, just on a different path. We did tell him that most women are way smarter than men, but leading is not their task. Ours is the important task of protecting from covert, reptilian attacks made by sinister and deceptive liars. Bad guys acting like good guys. That's what we good women detect. And we detected it right in front of us!

This disgusting poser couldn't keep his lying secret to himself. He actually broadcasted it as he pulled out of the parking lot at the snack shack. He drove an insanely out of place vehicle for the area. He drove a 2011 orange corvette and announced the word: SPOOKE. The American Heritage Dictionary defines "SPOOKE" as "a secret agent; a spy." Gotcha, lying poser! You couldn't help but brag! His stupidity was revealed even more as he pulled out of the snack shack. He scraped his front bumper and dragged it on the elevated pavement. We laughed as he revved his engine in his last ditch attempt to save his pride. What an effing spooke.

Tailed, Surveilled and Threatened

There is nowhere you can go to get rid of the federal surveillance once they have locked eyes on you. You are not free. We're here to tell you that it is all an illusion.

Even getting a cup of coffee at a local coffee shop will get you some major aggression from the stooges the feds hire. Stupid, ignorant, young doofuses setting up road blocks in parking lots and screaming obscenities have absolutely no power over us. We made the choice long before these illegals or brain dead men ever showed up in our lives that we would never back down from standing for the truth. Don't they know that we are willing to die for what we believe? They have no idea. Federal reserve debt notes motivate them. Our God and the rights He has given us motivate us.

Just dropping off mail at our local post office can bring down the wrath of this criminal empire. Walking and talking with love letters in hand can get the federal agents out in swarms, lying in wait and circling like vultures. It makes us think they are actually jealous. These men could not have known either a mother's love nor a devoted, insanely beautiful woman's love. So that is why they wait and stalk to harass and terrorize. It has the opposite effect on us and yet they still haven't learned that about us. We become more happy and more determined to walk the narrow road of life with our God, our love, our Barry, and our freedom. No turning back.

One day while we were outside working in the backyard we saw a strange, ginormous dark figure. He was wearing all blackish-navy clothing. He was standing ominously and staring. We stopped and stared back at him. After many minutes of this, we then took out our phone camera and snapped a picture of him. He then hid behind the trees. The man stalking us was not one of our neighbors, but a paid private contractor that our neighbors happily allowed on their property in return for a bank envelope filled with cash. Bank envelopes filled with cash lure soulless neighbors into gladly allowing government contractors on their property to stalk innocent Christian Constitutionalists and hide behind trees when caught. This is America.

On another day while delivering love letters to our Barry, we had an unwelcome and unconstitutional visit from a fed in a big black unmarked SUV. We had been airtagged before we left for our outing to the post office. Nothing new there. That's a daily event. This oversized, ugly, unloved, sold out piece of crap agent ran his ginormous truck up against our path alongside the brick post office, pinning us with little room to spare. My daughter was directly in front of me just a couple paces ahead. I never leave her side knowing that this sinister federal government hates her for loving Barry. This federal pig was sitting his fat obese rear end in a federal vehicle loaded with high tech gadgetry that filled the dashboard of the truck. He stupidly opened up his mouth and spoke to my beautiful, pure, young daughter and said, "You keep getting dumber and dumber every day, don't you." I immediately replied and told the big fat pig to mind his own business. When we got passed the vehicle, my daughter told me the exact words he spoke for her ears only. I turned in fury and screamed for the whole town to hear me and called him an effing fat slob. I gave him the double middle finger sign. He heard and saw me in his rearview. He was conducting no business at the post office. He was there to terrorize us, but instead triggered our fight response. He returned the hand gesture and moved on. That was the only smart thing that ugly, unlawful fed did.

Paid contractor on our neighbor's property hired to stalk us.

It's Unlawful!

The Postmaster took a step back in horrified disbelief. "She said what? She said that?" Yes. She did. Our report of stolen mail was not being resolved. The substitute mail carrier was not being questioned nor removed for the suspicious handling of our personal mail from Barry. My daughter witnessed the removal of the card Barry sent to me, legal correspondence was missing from another envelope, and seven months of mail from USP Florence ADMAX had not reached our mailbox.

We began our search by inquiring at the post office assigned to be the Distribution Center for the surrounding communities that receives and sends the mail, along with the handling of all the mail carriers. We had noticed our faithful mail carrier had been removed from our route when the mail began to go missing. Our brief conversation with the substitute carrier proved fruitless. He spoke inaccuracies and time line distortions of delivery to our residence. We watched his arrival at our mailbox every day for months and yet he said that he was only working our route for a few weeks. We confronted his lie yet he stuck to his story. He went on explaining that our mail was in a box, with a green card labeled, "Hold." He then called up our favorite and most faithful mail carrier to inquire about the "hold" box. "Why are you doing that?" my faithful mail carrier asked. It was a mystery as to why our mail would end up in some quarantine box in a mail facility. It was explained as a mix up, a misunderstanding, but the problem persisted and it still didn't explain why seven months of mail vanished into thin air. Why are they holding it and who put a hold on it in the first place?

This would not be resolved so it forced us to make an in-person visit to the postal distribution center in the next town. It would be an unpleasant inquiry. Federal employees are the worst people to deal with when they have a god complex and are doing things against the law. We explained the missing mail only to meet with indignation and excuses. We were told that the substitute carrier is "a good federal agent" and would never steal mail. FEDERAL AGENT? Oh, okay. Then the Postmaster added that if we wanted the mail in the box with the green card labeled "hold," we would have to go to an "off the beaten" trail post office. What the heck is this box doing in that old town? No way. We're not going there!

We told a friend who works for the post office and she told us that she has never heard of a hold box in that part of town. She said, "Don't go there. Women go missing in that corrupt, dirty little town." Yeah, the mafia is big out there. We don't want to go swimming with the fishes.

We get it. We exposed these agencies working together. The Bureau of Prisons with the Post Office employing a third party substitute mail carrier being paid to break the law. No scruples. No morals. No conscience. No accountability. No fear, because the agencies police themselves. Got it.

Here's the reports we filed on the repeated incidents with ZERO responses.

To: The Office of Inspector General

To: Postal Inspection Services

COMPLAINT FOR SEPTEMBER 29, 2024

Today, on September 29, 2024, I received an empty, unsealed envelope in my mailbox that was sent to me from the Attorney Grievance Commission. This piece of legal mail is marked as personal and confidential, and the envelope was open and the mail missing. I am Power of Attorney for my fiancé and have many legal duties to fulfill, and with my personal, confidential, legal mail being opened and stolen is not only criminal, but I am now unable to fulfill my legal duties, as I do not have the legal, confidential time sensitive paperwork to present to my fiancé, whom I represent. My legal paperwork has been stolen. This is the second time that this has happened. Once on August 10th, 2024 and now today, September 29, 2024. I now conclude that this must be theft from inside of the Post Office, as the mail that was stolen from me on two separate occasions came from two separate senders.

Why isn't the carrier questioned? Why isn't the Post Office checking the facilities as to when the mail went missing or if it came into the possession of the Post Office empty?

In addition, I have not received 5 months of mail from my fiancé, in which he writes to me daily. The letter carrier that K.S. called "D." said that whenever he has a letter to deliver from my fiancé, it is accompanied with a green card that says "HOLD" on it. So he places all of my mail from my fiancé in this box. K.S. then confirmed that there is a holding box for my fiancé's mail and this box is in O.F. (Out of town Post Office) My mail from my fiancé has been placed on hold and not by me, and I was informed that I am not able to cancel this hold. So I am also missing 5 months worth of daily letters.

COMPLAINT FOR AUGUST 10, 2024

On August 10, 2024 a new mail carrier came to deliver. I watch the mail come everyday, as I have extremely important legal correspondence that I am forced to rely on the Postal System to deliver. On that day, I received an empty, unsealed envelope, no mail inside of it. When I reported this about a dozen or so times, I told Postmaster K.S. about the suspicious behavior of this mail carrier, as he goes through my mail piece by piece, examining it and reading it as if it were his own mail. My mail only goes missing on the days he delivers. K.S. vehemently defended this letter carrier, saying that he is a new and a good federal agent that would never do such a thing, as if she could possibly know the conduct of a new employee. Remove the culpable staff and return my stolen mail to me.

I have reported this issue at least 8 times to K.S. and I've received no answers. That empty unsealed envelope went from towns like Denver Colorado, to Scranton, to Philadelphia, to Lancaster, to Archbald, all the way down to the carrier and I want to know why NOT A SINGLE person followed protocol, flagged that it was missing, and retraced the route. My mail was stolen and that's a federal offense. Why isn't the carrier questioned? Why isn't the Post Office checking the facilities as to when the mail went missing or if it came into the possession of the Post Office empty?

Feds in the Sky

(THE LITTLE CESSNA THAT COULDN'T)

It never ends. A constant flow of federal agents and paid contractors to spy on us and gather actionable intelligence on our peaceful, pure, uneventful lives. There is no end to their invasion of our privacy and rights to Life, Liberty and the Pursuit of Happiness.

It's happening in plain sight, people! Right in front of you while you move along in your day. Not only is the Air Force flying over our neighborhoods and homes in a constant poisoning of our air and land with their chemical sprays, it should be obvious to see the insane amount of flyovers that the feds have perpetrated over our peaceful home. From blackhawk helicopters to private Cessnas, all doing circles and repeated flights directly over the roof of our home, it is obvious that the feds have no problem spending many millions of taxpayer dollars to watch us feed our chickens and pull weeds from our flower beds! That should absolutely enrage you.

There is a particular little plane that the feds must have hired to flyover on weekends. By the way, our neighbor is pilot. Need we say more? It must really incite the sold out American that flies that little tin can plane for federal debt notes. We hold up a particular sign for him to read most every time he comes to do his surveillance. The sign reads, "FEDS WANT CROFT DEAD." We happily wave to him with our middle finger as he revs his toy plane's engine in retaliation.

One day in particular he was really feeling his "debbies" and he decided to do a strafing run on us. This is the kind of military exercise of attacking ground targets. Vietnam was notorious for this maneuver. He tried to be a paid mercenary with his little commercial Cessna, mimicking the strafing run of a U.S. B-57 Canberras! Poor little wanna-be. I'm sure if he could, he would....target us for demolition.

Don't get us wrong, many paid mercenaries fly over our home. A squadron of jets flew over one day in a four point formation while we were painting our colonial mural. A whole team of men were paid with your tax dollars to unzip their military pants. Unimpressed.

One evening while we were watching some programming on the scrying mirror (Television), a sonic boom took place right outside our window. All the lights were out in our home except for the glare of the paid programming. Suddenly, our room lit up with white light. Our eyes went to the window where a giant fireball formed. BOOM! We screamed, "AH-HHHHH!" The standing army strikes again! A sonic boom. Everything went back to normal, except the air tasted of static. The electrical charges left a bad taste in our mouths, but we went back to our scheduled paid programming.

On August 13, 2024 at 12:02 A.M, we were up and busy writing to our beloved Barry. We had the distinct feeling that we were being watched. While we wrote at our kitchen table, we angled our security camera monitor towards us, as we were already feeling very uneasy. After writing a few words we would look up at the monitor, and alas, a government orb circling our home. As this bright orb of light hovered, it did not bend as light usually does. It moved as one solid device, not passing through objects as a beam of light would do.

On yet another day they flew over some of their new demonic "alien" tech for our own private, VIP viewing. We yelled at the top of our lungs to get the attention of our brainwashed neighbors, but alas, no one gives a dung. We were so mad that they flew this thing over us. It was flat from our earthbound viewpoint. It was extremely large and moved slowly over us as we stood in our vegetable garden. Those criminals were curious to see if we'd freak out, run, hide, cry, or think aliens were here. No! It was the most criminal syndicate on the planet. The United States Military! Those corrupt pigs gassed up and flew over our little vegetable garden to terrorize us and all they got was a lot of profanity and middle fingers! All this alien crap is just that! A psychological operation on a population as dumb as a bag of rocks because they left the true and living God a long time ago. We're sure that thing was pouring out untold amounts of radiation on us. It doesn't matter. We will live as long as our Father, God, says so. When He calls us up for our next assignment to serve Him, we will be ready. There is no price too high to be paid for Father's glory. After all, this is His fight, not ours. He just included us in service. We will answer His call every time. No exceptions.

So these criminals in the federal government and military better think twice before hopping their little rear ends into their cockpits. They are stoking their own flames in the bowels of Hell every time they "just follow orders." And for those making these plans, we will see them at Father's throne where we will testify with the Angels and set our evidence before Father. We will be included in making their eternal sentence. Our little imaginations of their eternal torment can only go so far. Eye has not seen nor ear has heard the eternal torture and damnation they will receive because they have defecated on Father and the two women He loves. You have been warned. "Befehl ist Befehl" won't hold up with Father. He will roll up His sleeves and kick your behind into the eternal torment prepared especially for you.

A Busy 3 Weeks

The insane chain of events in our lives will shock you, so sit down. We don't want you to fall down. It started February 19, 2024, President's Day and we were hungry for Pizza Hutz pizza. Our old haunt in our small town had closed due to the lockdowns of 2020 and now we had to find another location. But where?

That day we Googled "Pizza Hutz Near Me" and we found one in a neighboring town. We decided we wanted to check their hours because of the holiday so we dialed the phone number listed and inquired. However, the "employee" didn't understand our question. We hung up the phone and decided to go in person to make our order to ensure a hot pizza.

When we arrived, it appeared to be a curbside only Pizza Hutz with extensive maintenance taking place. As we stood there, the whole crew in the back came out to inspect us. After a long wait, we got the pizza and we told the "employee" that we hoped to be back if he didn't poison it. He laughed and agreed with us. We knew this was not a pizza parlor. It was a front for criminal activity.

In the evening, we decided to check the day's call history on the "recents" tab under the phone app. We were checking the call times of our beloved Barry and to review the history of those calls. To our surprise, we saw an outgoing call logged into our phone history that we never dialed. It read 4:17PM, 42 seconds long to Ashland, PA. The only calls that were made that day were to Pizza Hutz and Momma.

We went into action. We called the Ashland number to see if it was Pizza Hutz. A foreign man answered the phone and said, "Pizza Hutz." We explained that we never called this number, yet it showed up on our phone as if we did. He explained that customers get transferred to other numbers all the time. He said his number was the Hazelton Pizza Hutz number. We then looked up the Hazelton Pizza Hutz number and it wasn't the same number. We called him back and he said to take it up with Pizza Hutz headquarters in Plano,Texas, which we did!

We then Googled the Pizza Hutz Headquarters in Plano, Texas and called it. A man named "P" answered the phone and said, "Pizza Hutz Headquarters, Plano, Texas." We gave him the Ashland, PA number and asked him to identify which Pizza Hutz that number belongs to. He replied that the number does not exist in the system as a Pizza Hutz number.

Now that "P" told us that the Ashland number is not a Pizza Hutz number, we tell him that this must either be a sex trafficking number, the federal government or both. We then ask him to repeat his headquarter location. "P" defensively replied, "I can't tell you that!" We then say, "Why not? You asked for our name and address." And "P" replied, "I can't tell you." Then we say, "Tell us because now we're thinking you're a fed and/or a trafficker." Then he blurts out, "Kansas!" We shouted at him, "You said Plano, Texas at first. You are lying!" "P" then says, "You realize that we are recording you right now?" Then we chime back, "Great because we're recording you too!" "P" then threatened us saying that he will contact law enforcement on us. He then said we will get a response from the corporation in 2-3 business days. Many business days later, nothing. We sent a notarized letter to the Pizza Headquarters in Plano, Texas and never received a response.

We decided to open our own investigation on this Ashland number. We researched it on an online phone book, and searched the number to find out it was a bandwidth (burner) phone number and not the Pizza Hutz at all! Worried that this was some sort of set up to create a phony plot, we decided to go to the police. After playing police ping pong, no law enforcement wanted to help us. We ended up at the police department located right in front of the Pizza Hutz. We used their emergency red "Bat Phone" because the police station was empty. So we waited. We were determined to get a report made to document the corrupt plot being created around us.

The Red Bat Phone

The next day we made a trip to the local police station. The station was empty. We located a "hot line," a kind of "Bat Phone" in the vestibule to call for an officer. The red phone sitting there was exactly like the Bat Phone hotline in the 1966 version of Batman. No dials on the red phone. It was in a dark solitary room with no officers in the police station. This was the last place we wanted to be because we had learned that calls to the police could not be made on our personal cell phones. We had to go to the station because our phones are blocked from calling 911. And forget about Googling non-emergency police contact lists. That comes up "forbidden" on our phones. The reason for that can be found in our book "Whitmer Kidnapping Hoax: A Plot to Kidnap Barry Croft Jr. Nameless Casualties Secret Wars."

Finally, we got a police officer dispatched to us where we explained the entire situation to Corporal M.S. The corporal took out his police phone to Google the Pizza Hutz number and we took out our phone to do the same. As Corporal M.S. was clicking through his screens he said under his breath, "F***!" We said, "What?" and he replied that he had never seen phone call logs changed before.

Our two numbers, Ashland PA burner phone number AND the listed number on Google as Pizza Hutz were two DIFFERENT numbers, and neither belonged to Pizza Hutz. Corporal M.S. confirmed this. He said that both of those numbers aren't Pizza Hutz. We concluded that our phones were giving us numbers that weren't the numbers we thought we were calling.

Corporal M.S. said, "Phone call logs can't be changed. I've never seen anything like this before." We disagreed with him. We had seen this before. When our Barry was arrested our phone call logs were deleted and texts vanished. Also, we had a voicemail placed into our phone that we never received on the day it was placed into our log. Tech can definitely be altered. No way is it reliable. He then asked for our I.D.'s and the research information that we had with us, along with the notarized letter we sent to the Pizza Hutz Corporation in Plano, Texas. We were glad to do so.

Corporal M.S. promised to look into it and get back to us the next day. He never did. When we see him on the road doing his job, he looks the other way. He's owned. He's a part of this now.

It happened again soon after our report to Corporal M.S. We tracked the number down that was planted into our phone. Another potential plot? Another false event? We know the feds and local law enforcement work together to commit crimes against innocent Americans that they target for knowing about the government's crimes. We did our homework. The web of deception is deep and the feds have been quoted to have said, "Don't let the facts get in the way of a good story." Wise up, Americans. You are being lied to. Oh, and we reported the Pizza Hutz number on Google as "spam." Google indicated it was reviewing our request but closed the case and the number remains, even though Corporal M.S. said it is NOT Pizza Hutz!

Rope

The tow rope worked wonders! No more unwelcomed fed visitors in our driveway, yard, or at our doors. The flow of paid fed contractors and even actual agents had to stop. They were not welcome on our property. They had no business bringing their ugly demonic faces to our door. The intrusion of our right to privacy must be stopped, hence, the rope.

We had put up surveillance cameras and no trespassing signs, but that still did not succeed at keeping these federal intrusions out of our lives. But before any of this went up, evil men and women were looking for us with their stupid faces asking stupid questions, just to dig for imaginary intel and gain access to our home and property. We were not buying their fake need to converse and learn from us.

Yes. Learn from us. One obviously fed woman thought we could teach her what we know about governmental corruption. We told her to buy our book, "Whitmer Kidnapping Hoax: A Plot to Kidnap Barry Croft Jr., Nameless Casualties Secret Wars," and do her own research. There is plenty of information in that book to last years in a pursuit of knowledge. She was indignant and rude. She resisted leaving our property. We told her to move out and pointed at the road. She took an inordinate amount of time leaving our driveway and so we said, "Leave. This is private property." She laughed. She's in the know. Technically, Americans own nothing. We signed the federal government's contracts and paid with their federal debt notes. Technically, they own everything, but the Constitution says the contrary. We wave that paper in their faces and we will die where we stand. She finally pulled out of our driveway. We still see her driving by.

So many strangers, pulling into our driveway, with so many inquiries. This has never been done before. We know hundreds of people in our community and the surrounding communities. We have lived a life of service, helping people out in times of crisis, welcoming them into our home for coffee and cake, hosting parties for friends, planning events for children to have fun and safe activities for seasonal holidays, hosting Bible studies, and yet, we never once had people just pull into our driveway asking us to teach them. Never. Human nature does not go that way. We have always sought to provide opportunities for people to realize that the hole in their lives could be met through a personal faith in God, not us. But now, all of a sudden, our driveway has become a highway.

A particular invasion on our property and home came from a man named P.B. who attended a small church we attended about 15 years ago. This arrogant man on a mission pulled into our driveway. He got out of his car and did not do the normal thing a person would do when in search of the homeowner. He did not go to our front door and ring the doorbell. No. We were in our kitchen and unaware of his approach. He decided to walk around the back of our home in our private space and approach our side door.

We found him leaning on our railing like an old, long lost friend of the family. Nothing could be further from the truth. He had found a family member in the back yard and started conversing about the good ole days at the small dead church when he knew us! At that time, my daughter was a preschooler, yet he was looking for both of us now.

Turns out I taught his step grandson in a children's Bible club. He was an uninvolved man that I never knew except in passing. He talked for a while to a family member who had no recollection of him and he went to the same church as us. As we assessed the situation, the unbelievable happened. We heard someone aggressively tugging on our screen door in the kitchen. The family member was not interested in pursuing a conversion with this stranger and left us alone to deal with this invader. Thank God we always lock our screen doors! This piece of crap scared the heck out of us. We would deal with this intruding third party fed contractor.

We were angry and said, "What do you want?" He explained how he knew us in vague terms and said that he was at our home one time for a party. It was nearly 15 years ago and no man has ever come to our door looking for us. They wouldn't dare. We are holy living women. This man was an unwelcome intruder.

We looked at him and said very deliberately, "We don't know you. Bye." We walked back into our kitchen and locked the door. We watched him leave. He stormed away and cursed angrily while pounding his fists towards the ground in obvious rage. It was exactly the manner of a paid federal contractor sent out to kidnap my daughter at a local coffee shop. These criminal hirelings are paid to gather intel and/or capture the target. Both of those fed contractors on two separate occasions left in a rage when their plans to accumulate more taxpayer wealth failed.

We would have loved to tell P.B.'s wife about his unsolicited visit to our home. On second thought, we're sure she knows the scoundrel she married. No man can hide that.

Can you see why we need a tow rope? The driveway must be roped off. But before we were able to block it, the worst was yet to happen. This next fed came to do some damage.

Feds at Our Door

Yes, you heard us right. Federal agents and paid third party contractors at our door. We will save their worst criminal act of attempted kidnapping for last. Let us tell you some of their criminality that is still shocking, but not as violently aggressive as their attempt to remove us off our property using law enforcement and the weaponized medical industry.

The audacity! There is no limit to the amount of subterfuge and distortions these criminals will expel to record and gather actionable intelligence. We were baking cookies or perhaps making dinner on this particular day when this paid third party contractor for a fusion center came to our door. He was too stupid to know that he was about to give up way too much information on himself. He went to our front door and rang our doorbell. He then walked away to approach our private side door. His odd behavior did not stop there. Not only was his recording device apparent to both of us, but when he knocked on our door looking for our book, he told such obvious lies. He said "Hello. I see you ladies are selling some literature." We told him to order it on Amazon. He'd rather buy it from us because he didn't know how to use those sites. We laughed at him. He told us his name was "M." We knew instantly that we'd find this idiotic fed online and find out why he really came to our door! My daughter has an eidetic memory and the most keen senses. We both knew he was sent from the Constable. We had his name, his face, and clothing, seared upon our brain. He looked like a sexual deviant and we kept our distance. We handed him a book and told him to do his homework. We spoke a few facts about the book and our love for Barry. He left having done his work.

Soon after this third party federal contractor left, we went to work. Our router burnt out right after we went to research him. Turns out that this evil piece of crap has a work page profile where he boasts of his titles. One of those titles include being a part of pizza corporate team in their loss prevention program. All these bastards work with PIZZA in some way! PizzaGate, anyone? These criminals have a torture chamber reserved for them in the bowels of where they will pay for their pizza crimes.

Mind you, these fed contractors are evil men. Feds hire men like themselves. This particular "M" is wrapped up in some degenerate behavior involving criminal charges of sexual misconduct with a fellow male Constable Deputy. "M" is a CLI, which he clarified on his own work profile. CLI is a "Command-line Interface" which is a means of interacting with a computer program by inputting lines of text called command-lines. This "Ethical Hacker" as he calls himself did some massively criminal things to our router and he hacked, unethically hacked, our phones and air tagged our vehicle. As soon as this "Law Enforcement, Security Management, Asset Protection, Cyber and OSINT Investigator, Ethical Hacker" left our property the network, "ESP_8CA975", showed up on our phones, and everywhere in our home. This network is an unknown open source in the place of our usual WiFi. "M" assumed we would be stupid like him. He thought we would click on that open source wifi and use it for his data collecting purposes. That didn't happen.

Did you get any of that? OSINT? That means "Open-source Intelligence, a collection and analysis of data gathered from open sources to produce actionable intelligence." Do you understand yet that our government is at war with its own people? "M" has a tremendous amount of law enforcement experience. or so he says, and the pizza corporate team is working closely with him! That should send shivers down your spine! Add to that the collection of "actionable intelligence." That tool is used by Fusion Centers. These centers are everywhere! Everywhere in the United States hiding in plain sight under many disguises like pizza parlors, police stations, constables, Mexican restaurants, the list goes on. In the English Dictionary the definition of actionable intelligence is this: "Military; the necessary background information that will enable someone to deal quickly and efficiently with a particular situation."

Our investigation turned up these facts: The neighboring county constable is a Fusion Center. "M" is employed by that Fusion Center. He planted an open source network into our cell phones via a stingray chip to gather intel on us. He burnt out our router. He didn't return because he knew we found him. Hide while you can, filthy fed! You forgot one thing. God is omniscient and He saw you. Your judgment is coming. You are guilty.

Since then, we discovered what "M" activated. It was a stingray equipped with a surveillance camera and microphone in the form of a chip. We searched for months to find out how "M" activated the ESP stingray in our home to collect data. That chip is located inside of our freeze dryer. Unplugging the freeze dryer resulted in disconnecting the stingray from its power source. ESP disconnected! This fed contractor for a fusion center had invaded our home. Warning. Anything that the government labels as a "prepper item" is riddled with surveillance. This China-made freeze dryer came equipped with USA government surveillance technology, waiting to be activated on unsuspecting, innocent Americans. Our government is at war with "We the People."

Attempted Kidnapping

We were outside painting and enjoying a beautiful day when someone in an unmarked police Interceptor pulled into our driveway.

It started a week prior when we received a suspicious text message on March 5, 2024 stating that a ride to our location had been requested. On March 5th, a Medical Sedan trip was booked for us to go to "Guise Singer" Behavioral Health. This specific psych ward was built through a joint venture partnership with one of the country's largest hospital systems to create one new 96 bed inpatient behavioral health hospital. It was confirmed and "Pocuton Transportation" was scheduled to pick us up at 4:15pm and we could directly contact them at 570-***-1363.

We were startled that this text came 4 days after speaking and making a report with Corporal M.S. This wasn't spam. This came from a legitimate phone number registered to a notification service network we'll call "One Way Trip" Health AND the number we were given to contact was a County CONSTABLE.

When the text message came through, we decided to watch from our third story attic window to see if they actually would come and attempt to kidnap us. We waited. It was a false alarm that we would later realize to be a story they were creating around us. They would reinforce their lie by sending us a text message to rate our overall experience with "Pocuton Transportation." "One Way Trip" Health wanted to know how well their federal contractors performed on our one way trip to the funny farm! Weaponized medicine and law enforcement working together as a joint agency task force.

One week later, the Constable was ready. They called us this time. And while the criminal act was in progress, our phone rang. At the precise time that the phone rang, an unmarked white police Interceptor pulled in our driveway. A man got out of the car and directly approached us. We grabbed the phone and answered it. The caller ID read "Healthcare California." We turned our attention to the fed contractor, possibly agent and said, "We don't know you. Leave our property." With no word of identification, he turned around as abruptly as he had approached. He got into his car and left. We stood and watched. He circled the block and passed our home about four times. Planes and helicopters were flying over our property all the while this was happening.

Now, back to the phone ringing, we answered it without a word. A lady immediately said, "D?" I said, "Sorry, wrong number." She wanted to speak and said, "Well...." We hung up the phone and didn't give her a chance to speak. We don't talk to feds. After the call was disconnected, we checked our call logs. The area codes didn't match up. We went to work researching the number that was left in our call logs from "Healthcare California." It turned out to be a local psych ward.

There could be no excuse for this action. #1 The local psych ward had OUR address and phone number. #2 Upon talking to and questioning the Executive Vice President Clinical Services Quality and Compliance, a man named B.C., gave us a few pieces of critical information. Our number was placed into their system via a man who went to the center and gave it to them not very long ago. AND, B.C. could not tell us if the Constable was involved. Our names, address and phone number were given to them at the psych ward and he could not deny that the Constable set up this appointment and pickup. Everyone we spoke to at the psych ward denied

"Pocuton Transportation" to be real. We researched it and found out it is an LLC in Mountaintop, PA. We even found a photo of the police Interceptor SUV utility vehicle in the driveway.

The phone log inputted the California Healthcare number as Healthcare Scranton PA. The information button revealed that it was the crisis services number for the local psych ward. We then went onto the Center's website and located the staff tab. We identified the man who came to pick us up. He drove the white unmarked police Interceptor.

This man is named B.I. He is, but no longer, the head of the behavioral center's department and transportation. The number that called us the very moment he pulled into our driveway belonged to the psych center where he was employed for 20 plus years! He is a part of the psych ward's Crisis Receiving and Stabilization Unit. This center receives police drop offs. It is an eight bed unit for people who present a risk to themselves or others. Medication is always in use for all who enter and it is an involuntary submission. That means you can kick and scream, but you are going there no matter what! No Constitutional Rights!

This man who came to our home had prior military experience. The police, psych wards, and veterans teamed up to take us against our will. We call that attempted kidnapping. We did some background work. We called the psych ward and they disavowed knowing anything. We contacted B.I. privately via letter. No response.

We were always taught that you die where you stand if anyone tries to take you away. That's what would have happened if they kidnapped us. The planes and helicopters were there to capture the whole thing. It didn't go down. We acted quickly and identified the criminals in our federal government in a joint agency task force. Turns out that B.I. is a neighbor. He is a man who has worked doing this criminality for 20+ years, and yet he has no phone extension or office, and no one at the psych ward is at liberty to say if he works there. And his family, living in our neighborhood, had no idea that he worked for the Center, let alone have a 20 plus year career there. We checked out the psych ward staff website, and B.I. is no longer listed as an employee.

Traitors, posers, sellouts, murderers. You wouldn't haven't even known if we were kidnapped, quarantined, force medicated and/or murdered. Psychology has been weaponized. This is what we mean when we say, "Nameless casualties. Secret wars."

> +1 (215) ███ 9702
>
> Text Message
> Tue, Mar 5, 2:16 PM
>
> Hi ███. A ride has been requested for you at 3:15pm EST on 03/05. We'll send you more information closer to the ride.
>
> Hi ███, the Medical Sedan trip you booked for Mar 05 to ███ ███ Behavioral Health is confirmed. Poc███ Transportation is scheduled to pick you up at 4:15pm EST, and you can contact them directly at (570) ███-1363

Note the number in which we have been directed to contact. (570) *** 1363. That is the constable's phone number. They sent the ride.

SUPERVILLAINS WITH BADGES 67

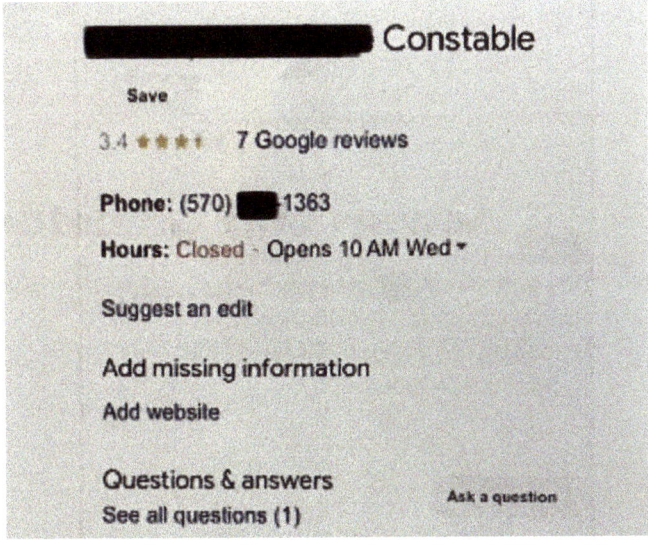

Notice the matching numbers. (570) *** 1363

Notice the phone number (215) *** 9702 matches with the number that sent us the initial contact.

WE'RE ON A HITLIST

+1 (804) ███ 7484

Text Message
Tue, Mar 5, 5:53 PM

███ trip here! Tell us about your ride with Poo██ Transportation . Rate your overall experience from 5 (excellent) to 1 (poor). Reply STOP to stop these texts.

This text was sent to us to confirm that we took a trip with the constable to the behavioral center which never happened. This was an attempt to set up a false scenario to kidnap us.

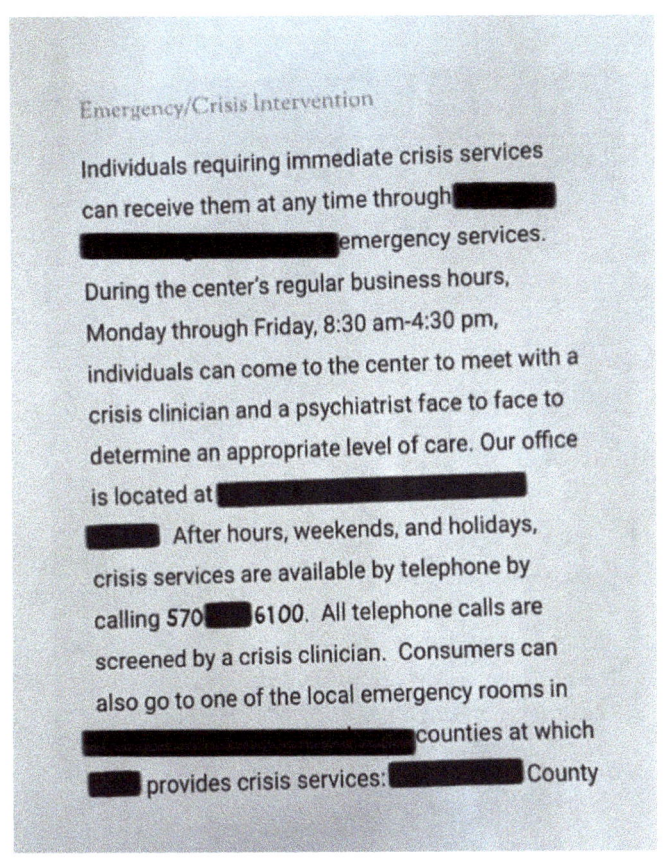

> Emergency/Crisis Intervention
>
> Individuals requiring immediate crisis services can receive them at any time through ▮▮▮ ▮▮▮ emergency services. During the center's regular business hours, Monday through Friday, 8:30 am-4:30 pm, individuals can come to the center to meet with a crisis clinician and a psychiatrist face to face to determine an appropriate level of care. Our office is located at ▮▮▮ ▮▮▮. After hours, weekends, and holidays, crisis services are available by telephone by calling 570 ▮ 6100. All telephone calls are screened by a crisis clinician. Consumers can also go to one of the local emergency rooms in ▮▮▮ counties at which ▮ provides crisis services: ▮▮▮ County

Note the phone number for the crisis service center, (570) *** 6100.

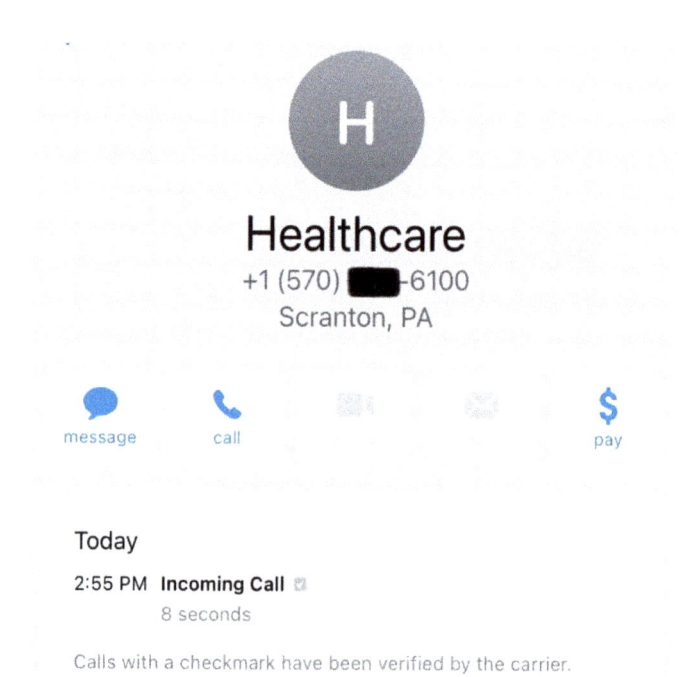

Healthcare
+1 (570) ███-6100
Scranton, PA

Today
2:55 PM **Incoming Call**
8 seconds

Calls with a checkmark have been verified by the carrier.

This number matches with the crisis service center number.

Feds Online

While in Gettysburg for a couple days, the feds intercepted a text that we sent to a medical researcher from the UK. An acquaintance of ours was looking to reach him and so we set out to help make that happen.

We found the doctor's verified account and messaged him our request and included some of our research on the United States Code. Both our acquaintance and the doctor did make contact with one another, but we paid a price for having reached out.

Facebook is actually FedBook. It is loaded with Federal Agents spying and collecting data from unsuspecting Americans. We knew this but it didn't stop us from trying to help someone in need.

We got a fed infiltrator, posing as the doctor. We knew instantly that it was no longer the verified account. It had been switched out. We were receiving a text from a criminal fed spying on us. We have included the actual text messages so you can see the depth of stupidity and the threats they are willing to make against innocent people. This particular idiot couldn't even speak. His threats are meaningless. His words are incoherent. Again, hiding on Facebook, intercepting and posing to be someone that he cannot even come close to imitating. We are light years above this reptilian Federal contractor. This was the beginning of the targeting by the feds. More proof that feds hire men like themselves. Stupid, lawless, brainless, morons motivated by paper federal debt notes destined for fire.

Every email we send out is labeled as "dangerous content." In other words, we are flagged. When an email is flagged, it is either intercepted by federal agents, informants, contractors, or it is marked as dangerous so that the recipient will not open it. Anytime we get a response from an email we send out it is always the federal government responding and not the addressee. Emails never get to their intended destination. Do you see why we need to make a PAPER trail? Technology can be altered and intercepted. Making a paper trail is the only sure way to expose the feds and deter them from adding to their criminality. We fill out forms and write these books to leave a papertrail in case we come up "missing." We broadcast what they do before they do it.

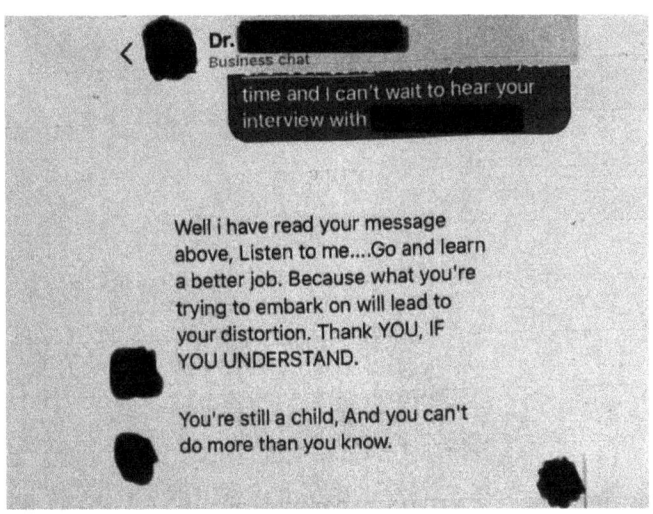

Feds flagging and intercepting contact with verified accounts.

Open Investigation

The Bureau of Prisons announced that an open investigation had been initiated against us for "nefarious and ill-gotten gains." You heard right. The lead FBI agent in the prison where Barry is kept in absolute solitary confinement made a glaring and unsubstantiated accusation against us. He told Barry to let us know that we are UNDER INVESTIGATION by the FBI. Why? Well, they don't need a reason. They do whatever the heck they want without accountability.

SIS (Special Investigative Services) Technician "Lizard," as we call him, slithered his way to Barry's double vaulted door and ranted about us putting money on Barry's commissary. He was super ultra enraged that we did not listen to him and stop sending money to sustain Barry. He would NOT send through any of the money to Barry's account that we had added but instead, steal it for the slush fund the BOP loves to keep in the black.

We would not obey the Lizard nor would we cower in fear and comply with his orders. We had a few ideas. Since Lizard blocked all money coming from anyone with the last name of "Nichols," we had one brave friend who stepped up and helped us. He put our money on Barry's account for us through Western Union. This enraged the Lizard! A new protocol must be made immediately for this lack of compliance to the random will of the psychopath in charge. Since our friend had helped us in our first book, "Whitmer Kidnapping Hoax: A Plot to Kidnap Barry Croft Jr. Nameless Casualties, Secret Wars," he was now included with us as among those who could not deposit money for Barry's commissary.

With this new invention of a non-existent protocol, we turned to a family member without the sinister last name of Nichols. And what do you think happened next? A new fake protocol! This person could not put money on Barry's commissary either. Why? Because he never wrote Barry a letter!

It was for this reason, SIS Tech Lizard opened up a full investigation on us. He invented the criminal accusation that we have nefarious and ill gotten gains to do such a criminal act as deposit money for a man who is our family!

We know why Lizard did this. Read on.

Why the Tyrants Rage

Lizard got caught with his pants down when he decided to storm into Barry's cell and threaten the only family Barry has that actually takes on evil. We went straight to work when we heard that our money would be blocked by the Bureau of Prisons and our Barry would suffer more deprivation, violating all his Constitutional Rights. He was experiencing "cruel and unusual punishment," an eighth amendment violation, and we set out to expose it.

We wrote up an extensive document using the Bureau of Prisons OWN handbook. They were committing infractions concerning their own policies! Seems that the paper trail of deception they produce in their handbook was being violated by the criminal employees that the agency hires. We sent our paperwork of THEIR infractions to the Director of the Bureau of Prisons, the Regional Director, BOP Headquarters in Washington, DC, the ADMAX Warden, and SIS Tech Lizard. We spelled out their criminal violation of the Constitution and their own handbook protocols!

It took 3 months for the chain of command to reach Lizard. But it did reach him. The Bureau of Prisons is trying to convince the public that it is actively seeking out violators of their policies and punishing their employees, but don't be fooled. It is all a facade. They do not purge their ranks, they only shuffle their agents around. They do not police their own criminality coming down from the ranks, even as high as Washington DC.

But this is what got the Lizard to temporarily cease-and-desist. The agencies HATE paper trails. We have documented their criminality every step of the way. Barry, Tessie, and I have filled out more forms, grievances, sworn and witnessed affidavits than we can count because it is in THEIR system that we confront them. For that,

"HE HATE US!"

No love loss for us. We hate tyrants and they come in many forms. Their favorite costume is that of "the good guys, the defenders of freedom" but they are actually Supervillains with Badges.

So why do these villains in charge surveil and hunt us down and even attempt to kidnap us in order to remove us from the planet? It has nothing to do with any crimes on our part. No. Lizard's full investigation uncovered our pure lives, free of all crimes. It doesn't have to do with our love for sewing, gardening or cooking. So why do they want to harm us? Simple. WE OPPOSE THEIR CONTROL. They will oppose and expose their CRIMINAL CONTROL. They will not stand for that. They will attempt to kill us and in that way they silence us. We threaten their cover of darkness and we expose the tyrants in charge of our country.

Every generation has to secure its own freedom. "You have a Republic if you can keep it." This is not a one and done kind of fight. The Demonic Tsunami backbuilds and strikes in every generation and if we are not willing to fight it and train our children and grandchildren to identify and resist luciferian control, then freedom will be lost and we will plummet into global tyranny. 1776 was just the birth of freedom! We have a Republic IF we can keep it!

We have a duty to secure our own freedom. We have a duty, at the very least, to make sure it exists for our children and grandchildren. It is a most egregious sin against God, your family, community and your country to do nothing and just let tyranny take over our lives.

We practice what we preach. Go and do likewise.

Epilogue

Before we sign off, we must tell you where your salvation lies from this all-consuming demonic tsunami of fascism. It has engulfed every facet of the federal government with its myriad of tentacles in its ever increasing agencies. It is armed to kill and its target is you.

Let us enlighten you. The whole stage is set in America for self destruction. Division and chaos is the American way. This is the federal government's tactic because as they incite division and chaos, they can then move in with the solution. It will always mean the loss of freedom and the imposition of tyranny.

You will succumb either through fear or brainwashing if you are not ready for the demonic tsunami crashing in on America. You will do exactly as you are told and believe every word spoken by those in control if you do not find the truth.

TRUTH. You must become a seeker of truth. You must step out of the mainstream and alternative lies and seek truth. You will not find it on your television set. You will not find it on your Google algorithms. Set your heart and mind to SEE. Really SEE. Start with our two books. There is MUCH to research. Look up into the sky and see the Air Force poisoning our air and land. Look at the grocery shelves and see them empty. Look at all the empty retail space and the dwindling workforce. Look at people with their vax injuries and their deadpan stares that have become the norm. Look at the social distancing still in place and the ineffective, demonic mask that covers the image of God in people He has created. Research the information we have given you in the two books we have written. You have work to do. You must seek the Truth. You will find the Truth if you search for it with your whole heart.

This is the River. It is the truth. Truth saves. Truth grounds and strengthens. While everyone else melts in fear, chaos and confusion, submitting to their torturers, you will have clarity, purpose, bravery and understanding. You will resist tyranny and be safeguarded because the truth has set you free from the fear of death and control.

Here's the first "sermon" we ever wrote to Barry. Now we will share it with you. Turn off the TV. Burn some midnight oil. Ask God to help you. He will. Afterall, He is the River. The truth will set you free.

Find the River

"Then the angel showed me the river of the water of life, as clear as crystal, flowing from the throne of God and of the Lamb down the middle of the great street of the city..." Revelation 22:1-2

Working out at a local gym is where it happened. It was October 2019. Earbuds in and spinning like hell on the elliptical, I was worshiping the LORD with the song by the Ball Brothers,"The River." All of a sudden, dimensions collided, and WHAM! A full salvo from the LORD hit His target and sent shock waves through my brain and heart instantly changing the landscape of my life from that moment on!

"A demonic tsunami is coming! Find the River!"

I literally went from the most ecstatic moment of joyful praise to the most profound burst of tears I have ever experienced. It rang in my head, deafening me, like the shots of gunfire at close range. God Almighty had made first contact. His air to surface missile had hit His intended target. My entire being had been captured. I would set out to find "The River."

On March 13, 2020 at 3:49PM the nation would receive a direct hit straight out of the fallen angel handbook. The offensive would strike terror in the heart of a nation no longer under God. My daughter had experienced the same offensive strike from Almighty God which awakened her and put her at attention. We stood together at the Rally Point and in position, standing by waiting at His go! It was at that precise moment on March 13 that Tessie Liz had spotted the fallen angel agenda and captured a live photo of the demonic tsunami planned to decimate a fallen Republic.

Never would I have imagined a free Republic capable of such treason on a free people! It sent me into a tailspin as I engaged the demonic forces through research and prayer. It was at that point, in early 2020, I would meet a man who had experienced the River and had it gushing out of him! He had the demonic tsunami three quarters of an inch off his ass and his 3% spirit was full on 100% of the time! He was among the true church, the Elect of God. He is the man God would inspire to start The Light of Liberty Church of God. But first he was making a full burnt offering of his life. He follows orders to a tee. His Commanding Officer is Jesus Christ. He would never defect no matter the cost.

By now you are asking who is this spirit of 1776 roaming among us? He became known to me as "The Gentleman from Delaware," Barry Croft. He is a Christian Constitutionalist with the truth of God gushing out of him. The River was a torrent in and through him. I was immediately drawn to his words. The Spirit of Christ testified this to be the truth

I was seeking. It answered all my questions and set me on a journey of the most intense research that lasted years!

The River was in the Gentleman from Delaware. Just as Christ had promised over 2000 years ago. He had gone back to the Father in order to send His Spirit! No longer would he just be among us, He'd be IN us! A Torrent! His Spirit would be a Torrent of power able to save the soul from the fallen angel agenda, the Demonic Tsunami.

Our country's Founding documents have been subverted by a whore, defacto document called the USC, the United States Code. Start studying, researching, praying and living free. The perpetrators of this coup in our country? Our own federal government in bed with a Globalist Agenda called Sustainability, Agenda 2030, Implementation 2024. America has become a junta society.

Roger that!
Demonic Tsunami has been engaged!
Meet at the Rally Point!
The River!
God Bless and Long Live the Constitutional Republic!
Theresa & Tess

Acknowledgements

The people we need to thank for the writing of this book are few, practically nonexistent. In all honesty, we actually have to thank our enemies for making this book possible. But before we do that, we must turn all our attention to God, our Father.

If it were not for the truth that God revealed to our minds starting back in 2019, we would have been in darkness and fear that the majority of Americans experienced. We would have viewed the virus hoax, the mask, the mandates, the destruction of businesses and the supply chain, the medical tyranny, the "forced" vaccinations to retain employment, the election selection, the riots, the Maui military nukes, the "controlled" FEMA burn in East Palestine, OH, the recent fake assassination attempts on candidate selection for the office of president, all as random events. But they are NOT random. These events are planned. Scheduled events courtesy of the red, white and blue. Once you know the truth, these events are not scary. They don't cause trauma and fear. And without the trauma and fear, the federal government has no power to control and take away our freedom. So, we want to thank God, our Father, for pouring upon us His River of Truth that has set us free from the fear of death. All glory goes to the Father and His eternal Son, Jesus Christ our Lord.

Now for our enemies. Thank you. You have played a significant role in bringing the will of God into our lives. Together we serve the Lord through your criminal terror and tyranny and find that God is, in fact, enough for us. No matter what you do to us, we will not back down from our duty and privilege to serve the Living God. We will cling to and proclaim the truth in this earthly dimension for as long as our Lord sees fit. He calls the shots. You do not. All that's left to say to you is, "TheLord rebuke you."

About the Authors

Theresa Nichols:

I am a Christian Constitutionalist. It is for this very reason the American government, with its sinister agents in the FBI, have targeted my daughter and I for demolition.

Loving and supporting Barry Croft Jr. has cost me the security of my daughter, my life, and my property. No one can speak the truth in this country without risking their own lives and the lives of those they love. The path of truth can get you killed. Jesus proved that with certainty. We are on the same path that He trod before us. We follow in His steps.

I speak the absolute truth in this book about what the federal government has done to surveil, terrorize and eliminate us. I remain unmoved.

Tessie Liz Nichols soon to be Croft:

I am a Christian Constitutionalist. That alone has put me on the top of the government's hitlist.

Having provided a home and family for my Barry, it has enraged the government to the point of wanting to eliminate me. As the targeting worsens, I celebrate, because it proves that my beloved Barry's deliverance draws near.

In faith, I continue to bake, sew, write, cross stitch, and pray for my Barry. Nothing this corrupt government can do will ever stop me from loving and comforting him, my Gunboat, my hero, my king, my husband to be. Destination known, baby.

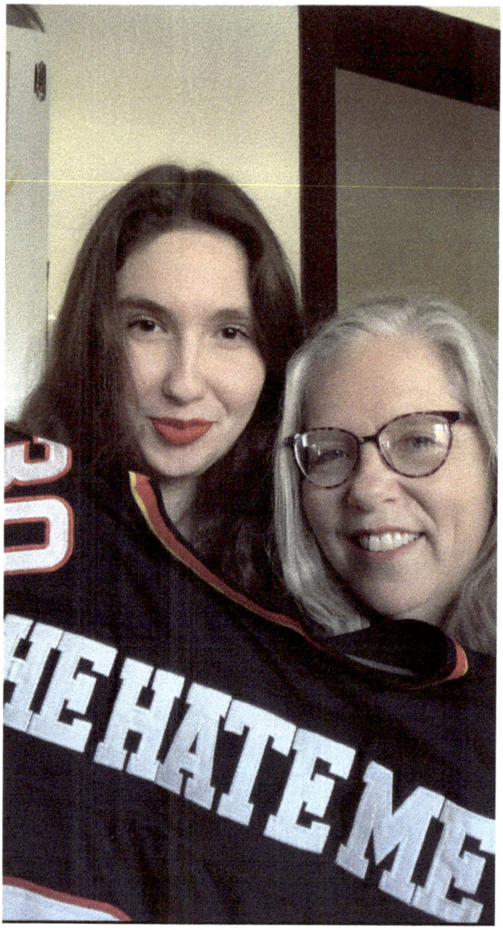
30
HATE ME

Milton Keynes UK
Ingram Content Group UK Ltd.
UKHW020837061224
452240UK00010B/563